Can I know God?

ons we can ever ask. I am
sts?" because the human
People look up at the sky,
ous of something beyond
d, even if their view is that
here is no God. My friend had a daughter-in-law who was a devout atheist. One day she was very angry and said to him, 'I hate your God. I hate Him.' At least she believed in God even though she hated Him!

Did you know that you were created to have a loving relationship with God? It is one thing to believe that God exists, but it is another thing altogether to say that you KNOW GOD. You may know things about God, but do you know Him intimately? Do you have a personal relationship with Him? The Bible says that God can be known.

How can we know God?

We recognize degrees of knowledge of our fellow-men. We know them, we say, 'well', 'not very well', 'just to shake hands with', 'intimately', or perhaps 'inside-out', according to how much, or how little, they have opened up to us. Thus, the quality and extent of our knowledge of other people depends more on them than on us. Our knowing them is more directly the result of their allowing us to know them than our attempting to get to know them.

Man, by his own efforts, has not been able to get to know God, and will never be able to know God, unless God makes Himself known. But does God wish to make Himself known? Since He created us, is it not probable that God wants us to know Him? How might He bring this about? Often a simple illustration helps us to understand some deep truth...

If a skilled carpenter, who lived far away, wanted to introduce himself to us, what might he do?

(1) First of all, he might make a beautiful table and send it to us as a sample of his knowledge and skill. We would say, 'the carpenter who made this is a master craftsman. He pays great attention to detail. He clearly loves beauty, since he has made the table as beautiful as possible.' By studying the table we would learn a little about its maker.

Has God made Himself known to man in this way? Yes! God's wisdom and power are seen everywhere in nature. Every day science reveals more of the wonders of the created universe. As David the prophet says, "The heavens declare the glory of God and the firmament (sky) shows His handiwork" (Bible, Psalms 19:1). When we see the beauty and harmony of God's creation, and the intricate design of the smallest creature, we are moved to say, 'O Lord, how manifold are Your works! In wisdom You have made them all. The earth is full of your possessions" (Bible, Psalm 104:24). Since the world which God has created is wonderful, how much more wonderful must the Creator be! Surely everyone who uses his eyes and mind must realize that there is a God, and that God is great and wise and mighty. But there are many things about Him which we cannot know simply by looking at nature.

(2) Secondly, if the carpenter wished to tell us about himself, **he might write us a personal letter**, introducing himself and explaining how he made the table. The carpenter could send the letter with close friends. The friends could tell us more about the carpenter, such as where he lives, how old he is, how large a family he has and what he is truly like. So we would feel that we knew him much better than when we had only seen the table.

Has God written to us? Yes, 'the Holy Scriptures' (the Bible) are letters from God to mankind. He sent prophets to deliver His messages. In these writings God tells us about Himself and about His plan for humanity. The Bible is not the word of men but the word of God. The human writers of the Bible were inspired by God to write down exactly what He intended. So, when we wonder what God is like, we don't need to guess. We can go to His revelation, the Bible. There He tells us about Himself.

Here are some things which God reveals in His letter to us.

God is very great

God is infinite. He is far greater than everything He has made, far greater than anything that exists. As far as power is concerned, He does whatever He chooses (Bible, Psalm 135:6). Nothing that He chooses to do ever fails to happen (Bible, Isaiah 46:10). Nothing can resist His will.

As far as knowledge is concerned He knows every single thing (Bible, Psalm 139:2-5; 1John 3:20). He even knows your secret thoughts! Our knowledge is small and limited. We can only focus on one thing at a time. But that is not true of God. He knows all things at once as if they were happening in front of Him. There is nothing of which He is not aware. His understanding is unlimited.

God is *present everywhere*. Just as God is unlimited or infinite with respect to power and knowledge, so He is unlimited with respect to space. He is present at every point of space with His whole being. It is not that a part of God is in one place and a part of Him is in another. God Himself-the whole of God- is present wherever we go. This is difficult for us to imagine. Our mortal and finite minds cannot comprehend it.

> " 'Am I a God near at hand,' says the Lord, 'And not a God afar off? Can anyone hide himself in secret places, so I shall not see him?' says the Lord. 'Do I not fill heaven and earth?' says the Lord" (Bible, Jeremiah 23:23-24).

God's omnipresence is beautifully expressed by the prophet David,

> "Where can I go from Your Spirit? Or where can I flee from Your presence? If I ascend into heaven, You are there. If I make my

bed in hell, behold, You are there. If I take the wings of the morning, and dwell in the uttermost parts of the sea, even there Your hand shall lead me, and Your right hand shall hold me" (Bible, Psalm 139:7-10).

There is nowhere in the entire universe, on land or sea, in heaven or in hell, where one can escape from the presence of God.

As far as *time* is concerned, God is eternal. "From everlasting to everlasting, You are God," said David in Psalm 90:2. Everything owes its beginning to God, but He Himself had no beginning. He sees all time equally and vividly. In the New Testament, the apostle Peter tells us, "that with the Lord one day *is* as a thousand years, and a thousand years as one day" (Bible, 2 Peter 3:8). These verses help us to imagine the way in which God sees time.

God is absolutely *independent* and self-sufficient. He does not need any part of His creation in order to exist or for any other reason.

> "God, who made the world and everything in it, since He is Lord of heaven and earth, does not dwell in temples made with hands. Nor is He worshiped with men's hands, *as though He needed anything,* since He gives to all life, breath, and all things" (Bible, Acts 17:24-25).

God is *unchangeable*. He is always the same.

> "Of old You (God) laid the foundation of the earth, and the heavens *are* the work of Your hands. They will perish, but You

will endure; yes, they will all grow old like a garment; like a cloak You will change them, and they will be changed. But You *are* the same, and Your years will have no end" (Bible, Psalm 102:25-27).

Referring to His own qualities of patience, long-suffering, and mercy, God says, "For I *am* the LORD, I do not change" (Bible, Malachi 3:6).

God is Unique

God is Holy. 'God is light, and in Him there is no darkness at all" (Bible, 1John 1:5). The prophet Moses sang these words to God, "Who is like You, O Lord, among the gods? Who is like you, glorious in holiness?" (Bible, Exodus 15:11). God's character is perfect. He is pure and entirely free from wicked and dishonest motives, thoughts, words and actions. It is this characteristic which separates Him, and marks Him out as different from all His creatures. God's eyes are too pure to look on evil; He cannot tolerate wrong (Bible, Habakkuk 1:13).

God is righteous. He always does what is right. God is love. He is slow to anger and abundant in mercy and kindness. He is good, just and wise.

God is incomprehensible

Man's need is to get to heaven and to be with God, not to be able to plot heaven on a map or produce a concept of God that can be reduced to a statement on a postage stamp. Because God is infinite and we are finite and limited, we cannot comprehend Him. In this sense, God is *incomprehensible*. I am not saying that God cannot be understood at all. What I mean is that God cannot be *fully* or *exhaustively* understood.

The prophet David says, "Great *is* the LORD, and greatly to be praised; and His greatness *is* unsearchable" (Bible, Psalm 145:3). God's greatness is beyond searching out or discovering. His thoughts are so much higher than ours. "Great *is* our Lord, and mighty in power. His understanding *is* infinite" (Bible, Psalm 147:5). Similarly, when thinking of God's knowledge, David said, "*Such* knowledge *is* too wonderful for me; it is high, I cannot *attain* it" (Bible, Palm 139:6). "Oh, the depth of the riches both of the wisdom and knowledge of God! How unsearchable *are* His judgments and His ways past finding out!" (Bible, Romans 11:33).

We can never fully understand a single thing about God. His greatness, His understanding, His knowledge, His wisdom, judgment and ways are all beyond us. It would be easier to pour the entire ocean into a little cup than to grasp the greatness of God with the human mind.

These are some things which God has told us about Himself in the Bible.

How else has God made Himself known?

So far, we have seen two ways in which God has revealed Himself. First through Creation and secondly through His Holy Word, the Bible. Has He made Himself known in a clearer way? Yes. Let's return to our carpenter friend and see how else he might introduce himself to us.

(3) If the carpenter really wanted us to know him, what could he do? **He could pay us a visit.** He could surprise us by knocking at our door! We would welcome him, talk to him, and get to know him face to face.

So if God wanted to make Himself known to us as completely as possible, what would He do? Surely He Himself would come to live with us! God has, to some extent, revealed Himself to us by showing us His wonderful works in nature, by sending us the prophets and by giving us the Holy Scriptures. Yet we desire to know Him better.

But is such a thing possible? Could the Most High God live on earth among sinful men? Since we believe that God created all things, we say that He is Almighty and therefore nothing is impossible for Him. So if He wished to reveal Himself to men He would certainly be able to do so. To say that God could not do this would be to deny His almighty power, and that would be blasphemy. Yes, if He so desired, God could come and live with men so that we could know Him intimately!

The question is, did God want to visit us? Now I have good news for you—God was so eager for us to know and love Him that, in His infinite mercy, He came to live with men!

About 2000 years ago God caused His Light to shine into our world in a special way. The Light of God, who is also called the Word of God, clothed Himself with humanity in the womb of the Virgin Mary, and Jesus Christ was born. John (one of Jesus' disciples) wrote, "In the beginning was the Word, ...and the Word was God ...And the

Word became flesh and dwelt among us" (Bible, John 1:1, 14). "God was manifested in the flesh" (Bible, 1 Timothy 3:16). Jesus was truly man, since He was born to Mary. All that is in man was in Him -except sin. But He was also higher than man, since He was one with God. Therefore the coming of Jesus Christ into the world was truly the coming of God among men. This is clearly seen from His title 'Immanuel', which means 'God with us'.

Fully God – Fully Man!

The Bible is full of indications that Jesus was God on earth. He was called what only God is called. He was like what only God is like. He acted as only God acts. He claimed what only God claims.[2] Jesus Christ did not merely tell people about God, as the prophets had done. Rather, He revealed God to men because He was the perfect manifestation of God. One day Jesus said to His disciples, "If you had known Me, you would have known My Father also; and from now on you know Him and have seen Him." When Philip (one of Jesus' disciples) heard this he said, "Lord, show us the Father, and it is sufficient for us." Jesus replied, "Have I been with you so long, and yet you have not known Me, Philip? He who has seen Me has seen the Father; so how can you say, 'Show us the Father'? Do you not believe that I am in the Father, and the Father in Me? " (Bible, John 14:7-10). Some qualities of God, such as wisdom and power, are seen in nature. But in Jesus Christ the thoughts, purposes and acts of God (such as purity, holiness, love, justice, forgiveness of sin) are revealed in an incredible way.

God revealed Himself perfectly in Jesus Christ, so that all who wish to know God and come close to Him can find Him in Christ. It is written, "God, who at various times and in various ways spoke in time past to the fathers by the prophets, has in these last days spoken to us by His Son" (Bible, Hebrews 1:1-2). Many seekers of God have said, 'We did not know God until we came face to face with Him in His Son Jesus Christ.'

Did God cease to be God when He came in the form of man?

No! God spoke to the prophet Moses from a burning bush. Did He stop being God when He spoke to Moses? Of course not. God cannot be limited by anything. When God revealed Himself in the form of a man, He was not limited by that humanity. He continued to rule the universe. He continued to be what He always had been (God), but in Jesus He also became what He had never previously been (man). Jesus Christ was not 50% God and 50% man. He was 100% God and 100% man. Fully God and fully man. The divine Person took upon Himself a human nature. We can't really understand the mystery of how this happened. But it is conceivable, certainly, that God has the power to add to Himself a human nature and to do it in such a way as to unite two natures in one Person.

Here's an illustration to explain this: Imagine a brilliant light. Now imagine that the light is put inside a glass. Does the glass stop the light shining? No! In fact, as the light is reflected by the glass, it shines even more brightly. In a similar way, when God became man in the Person of Jesus Christ, the body did not stop Him being God. Jesus said, 'I am the light of the world.' God became what He had never previously been (man) but He continued to shine and to rule the universe. In this way, He revealed Himself to the world *more clearly*.

What was the real reason that God came in the likeness of men?

Why did God have to become man? What was the point? This is a very important question. It goes to the heart of Christianity. Yes, God revealed Himself to us in the Person of Jesus, but was that His sole purpose for coming in the likeness of men? To know the answer, we must go back to the beginning of creation. We need to grasp what happened in the Garden of Eden.

How did it all begin?

Everything about the world that God made was good. There was plenty of food and drink for every living creature. In this lovely setting the first people, Adam and Eve, lived. God told them that as long as they lived for Him, obeying Him, they would live forever, but that if they disobeyed Him they would surely die.

God wanted them to be His worshippers and to look after the earth and everything in it. God gave them a precious gift: free will. He did not make them like robots or machines so that they would have to love and obey Him. Love must come freely. This gift of free will was one of the main differences between humankind and the animals. Adam and Eve could choose between right and wrong, good and bad. They could choose to love each other or not, to do what God wanted or what they wanted, to live for God or for themselves.

They chose to disobey God. They preferred to please themselves rather than God.

Why did they do this? What went wrong?

All evil and wrong come from the devil. Even the word 'devil' has the word 'evil' in it. While everyone today believes that evil exists, belief in a personal devil has declined. Isn't he just a comic figure with horns and a curly tail?

The Bible tells us to take the devil seriously. It tells us that, far from being a comic figure, he was once a glorious angel in heaven. His name then was Lucifer, which means 'one who bears light.' He became proud and jealous, wanting to be like God. He was banished from God's presence and now does all he can to turn men and women against God.

It was the devil, Satan (a name which means 'the deceiver'), who tempted the first man and woman to choose wrong and disobey God.

So in this way sin and wrong entered into our world and into human life.

At first Adam and Eve had walked with God in a loving relationship. But when they disobeyed, sin formed a vast, insurmountable chasm between them and God. We call this 'spiritual death'. It is because

Adam became spiritually dead that he died physically several hundred years later.

As a result of what happened in the Garden of Eden, all of us are born with an infinite gap between us and God. Think of it like a box of dominos. You can stand them all up in a long line. If the first one falls down what will happen to the rest? They will all fall too. In the same way when the first man fell all the rest of humankind fell too. The prophet David wrote, “Behold, I was brought forth in iniquity, and in sin my mother conceived me” (Bible, Psalm 51:5).

This is very true! Think about children. One of the first words little children pronounce is ‘no’! We all know their very early disobedience. Does anyone teach them how to be naughty? Do you think children need to be taught how to disobey? Of course not!

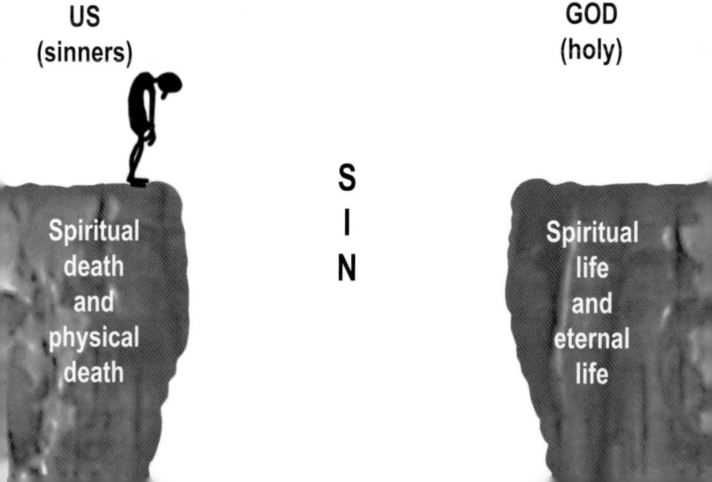

Parents teach them good behavior, but no-one needs to teach them naughtiness. By nature they know how to be naughty! It's in them from birth. What the prophet David said is absolutely true - we are born in iniquity, and in sin our mothers conceived us!

God is holy and we are sinful, so we are cut off from Him. "Your iniquities have separated you from your God, and your sins have hidden His face from you," (Bible, Isaiah 59:2).

Because people listen to the devil's lies, they go his evil, selfish way. It is this that causes all the crime and wrong and suffering in the world. This is why there is so much evil, so many broken relationships, so much selfishness and greed. We are all by nature self-centred rather than God-centred. There is no exception to this, "for all have sinned and fall short of the glory of God" (Bible, Romans 3:23). It is a disease we all have and it affects not just us, but everyone we come into contact with. The Bible calls this sin. This is what is wrong with the world, and that includes you and me.

By nature we are separated from God. It is our disobedience which separates us. Every man is sinful at heart; though someone may seem to be very holy outwardly, there remain sins of wrong motives, sins of the mind.

What is the solution?

Is there any hope? Many people try to bridge the gap by their own efforts. Some think they can get to God by being good religious people. They hope that their good deeds will outweigh their bad deeds enough to get them into paradise. But they never succeed. No one is perfect. It is not even that their contribution 'nearly but not quite' reaches God. The reality is that we fall infinitely short of the requirements. We can never reach God's standard by our own efforts. No matter how righteous we try to be, we are condemned, "for whoever shall keep the whole law and yet stumbles in one point, he is guilty of all" (Bible, James 2:10). Our sins can never be forgiven by striving toward self-righteousness. The huge chasm between us and God is still there.

The question remains; what is the solution?

Once, when I was sitting quietly, I saw a troop of ants marching up and down a wall. They were trying to carry a grain of wheat to the top. But without success. The grain of wheat was too heavy. The pull of gravity was greater than their efforts! I pitied them. I wondered how I could help those hopeless ants. If I had reached down with my hand, I might have squashed some of them by mistake. They would have run away in fear. I could not help them. The only way I could have helped them was by becoming an ant, while keeping my human strength! Only that way could I help without terrifying them.

We are a bit like those ants. We can never reach God by our own efforts and good works. The gravity of our sin is too great. It is stronger than our efforts. Sin weighs heavily on our shoulders. But God pitied and loved us. To liberate us from the tyranny of sin, He came in our likeness. He came as a man, but lived without sin. That was the main difference between Him and us. Who can re-establish the broken relationship between God and man? Surely, the only one who can bridge the gap is One who is both God and man.

My sins are not serious!

Let me tell you about what happened to a friend of mine. His name is Olivier. When he told me that he once went to prison for failing to pay parking tickets, I asked**,** *"why didn't you just pay them***?"**

He answered, "They were just 'parking tickets;' it was no big deal."

Then he told me that the police arrived at his home at 4:00 am, put him in a van and took him to court. As he stood before the judge, he said, "Your honour, I have brought 500 francs with me to pay the tickets and to cover the court costs."

The judge said, "Monsieur Argaud, I'm going to save you all that money. *You are going to jail*!"

Olivier was terrified.

His big mistake was that he trivialized his crimes by thinking that they were "just" parking tickets, and so he deceived himself. Had he known the judge's ruling (that he would go to prison), he would have immediately made things right between himself and the law.

Most of us realize that we have broken God's Law, the Ten Commandments, but we think it's no big deal. So, let me ask you a few questions about the Law you have broken and see if it is a big deal.

Have you ever lied? You say, "Yes. But they were only white lies. They were nothing serious."

Have you ever stolen something? You say, "Yes, but only little things."

Can you see what you are doing? You are *trivializing* your crimes, and like Olivier, you *will* deceive yourself. What you are doing is saying that you haven't actually "sinned." But the Bible warns, "He who says he has no sin *deceives* himself." The truth is that if you have lied, then you are a liar. If you have stolen anything (the value of the item stolen is irrelevant), you are a thief.

What you need to hear is the judge's ruling for lying and stealing. Here it is: "All liars will have their part in the lake of fire" (Bible, Revelation 21:8). All liars go to hell and no thief will enter heaven. Not one (Bible, 1Corinthians 6:9).

Now look at this: Jesus said, "Whoever looks at a woman to lust for her has already committed adultery with her in his heart" (Bible, Matthew 5:28). Have you ever looked with lust? Then you have committed adultery as far as God is concerned. Have you used God's name as a curse word to express disgust? If you have, then you have used His holy name in vain. That's called "blasphemy," and it's very serious in God's sight.

So if you have been honest enough to admit that you have broken those commandments, you are a self-admitted lying, thieving, blasphemous adulterer at heart. If God gives you justice on the Judgment Day, you will be guilty and end up in hell. Think of it - if you died right now, you would end up in hell... forever. So, what are you going to do? How can you make things right between you and the Law?

Can religion help?

Absolutely not!

There are millions of people on this earth who have never seen the serious nature of sin. They are in the dark about the Judge's ruling. They have no idea that they will end up in hell for crimes that they consider trivial. They know that they have to face God after death, but they think that their religious works (like Olivier with his 500 francs) will buy their way out of any trouble in which they may find themselves. And as long as they trivialize their sin, they will deceive themselves into thinking that they can work their way into heaven by their religious works. It is as futile as a man who tried to row against the river. He was in a boat caught in fast-moving water, heading for a massive waterfall with jagged rocks 150 feet below. A passerby saw him rowing against the current, but his efforts were futile. Minute by minute he was drawn closer and closer to the roaring falls. The passerby ran to his car, grabbed a rope from the boot and threw it to the boat. When it fell across the bow, he shouted, "Grab the rope. I will pull you to the shore!" He couldn't believe his eyes, for the man in the boat took no notice. He just kept on rowing frantically against the current, until he disappeared over the edge of the falls to his death.

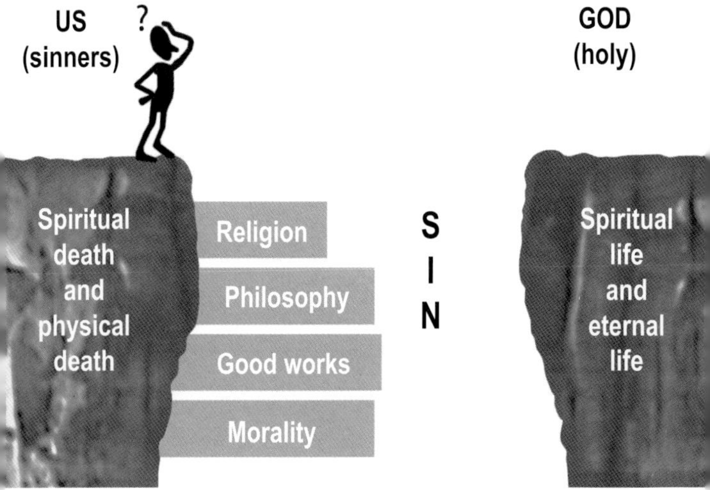

God Himself has thrown us a rope in Jesus Christ. He is the only One who can save us from death and hell. But we must let go of our own efforts to save ourselves and take hold of the rope. The moment we cease our own religious "rowing" and have faith in Jesus, we find peace with God. The Bible says, "For by grace you have been saved through faith, and that not of yourselves; it is the gift of God, not of works, lest anyone should boast" (Bible, Ephesians 2:8-9).

Let me give you another illustration to show that religion can never save you. Imagine that one day you go swimming and jump into deep water. You find yourself in trouble. Drowning! You are dying, but you cannot save yourself because you do not know how to swim.

You are hopeless and helpless. Someone approaches and yells, 'Pull yourself together and save yourself! Come on mate, do it yourself!' What a terrible thing to say to a drowning man! A second person arrives on the scene and actually jumps into the water. He starts swimming. He says, 'Look at me. Learn how to swim and do the same. Then you will save yourself'. How ridiculous! There is no time for you to learn. In fact, a drowning man is absolutely incapable of learning anything. Now a third person approaches. He dives into the pool, grabs you and drags you out of the water. You might resist him, but out of compassion he saves you from death. Now, which one of these three people would you thank the most? Surely the third one.

Religion is like the first two people. By nature we are drowning in our sin. We are in a mess because of our separation from God. Religion tells us, 'Save yourself. Do this and that. Don't do this or that and you will be saved.' Some religious leaders are seen as examples. Their followers are told that if they imitate their lifestyle, they will be saved. It is like the second person who jumps into the water.

So religion cannot save us. We are hopeless. The Bible says that we are incapable of saving ourselves. That is why we need someone to jump into the water of our life and get hold of us and save us from our sin. This is exactly what God has done. God says to us, 'I know your situation. I know that you are separated from Me. I know that your life is in a mess. I know that you cannot save yourself. And I know that giving you laws and commandments will not save you because you can't and don't do them. You are incapable of fulfilling them. But,

I will come to where you are and get you out of the tyranny of your sin.' So God came to this world in the Person of Jesus Christ. "Christ also suffered once for sins, the just for the unjust, that He might bring us to God," (Bible, 1Peter 3:18). When Jesus died on the cross, He died as our perfect human substitute. He took the punishment that we deserve for our sin. He bridged the insurmountable chasm that separates us from God.

It is unwise to reject God's saving plan. What do you think of the drowning man who refused to be saved?

When someone allows Jesus to save them (by trusting in His death and resurrection), Jesus forgives their sin and grants them a place in Paradise. He will dismiss the case against them.

Why was Jesus' death necessary?

Let us get it clear that Jesus was dead. Dead beyond any shadow of a doubt. He was certified as dead by the centurion in charge of the execution squad. He was recognized as dead by Pilate, the governor (who gave permission for a friend to bury His body). And the crowning proof is that when a spear was thrust into His side under His heart in order to make sure He was dead, out came what an eyewitness called blood and water (Bible, John 19:34f). Obviously the scientific explanation of this was unknown to men of those days, but the diagnosis is clear. Dark blood and light serum came from the body of Jesus, and the separation of clot from serum in the blood is the strongest medical proof that the patient is dead.

So don't swallow any of the "swoon" theories which imagine that Jesus was not quite dead but recovered in the cool of the tomb! He was dead all right.

But why did Christ need to die? Could He not have saved us without dying? Man had broken God's law and the penalty was death; physical and spiritual. "The wages of sin is death." (Bible, Romans 6:23) How could Jesus Christ deliver us without meeting our full penalty?

Death is man's big problem. If anyone was to save us, he would have to resolve this problem. He would have to conquer death. He would have to restore our broken relationship with God.

When Adam and Eve disobeyed, God immediately promised to send them a Saviour. Through that Saviour's suffering, people would be saved.(Bible, Genesis 3:14-15; Isaiah 53) In fact, the Bible says that "the Lord was pleased" to offer Christ as a sacrifice for man's sin. (Bible, Isaiah 53:10)

A judge sat in the courtroom, wearing his judicial robe. A young girl stood before him. She had been charged with driving without a license and speeding down the highway. The penalty for these charges was two thousand pounds. He pointed his finger at her and asked, *"Are you guilty or not?"* to which she answered, *"Yes. Your Honor, but I cannot afford to pay the penalty."* The judge simply said, *"You must pay,"* and then closed court. He stepped down from the bench, took off his robe and gave the girl two thousand pounds. Why? Because he was her father. He could not dishonor his name by letting her go

free, but he was also merciful and loving and could not bear to see her put in jail because of her inability to pay. The only solution, therefore, was for him to pay the penalty himself.

In the same way, Christ has paid the penalty for our sin. God is holy. He hates sin, so He cannot simply close His eyes to our disobedience. Because He is a just and fair God, He must punish sinners. Death is our penalty; spiritual death, physical death, then ultimately, eternal separation from God. No mere man could ever pay that penalty for us. But in His mercy, God decided to pay the penalty Himself so that we can go free. Jesus Christ, being equal with God, took off His robe of heavenly glory and came down to earth as a man. On the cross, He was punished for our sins. The justice and mercy of God came together, and both were satisfied.

Without Jesus' death there would have been no way for us to escape God's punishment for our sin.

What is the evidence that Jesus' death was sufficient for man's salvation?

The evidence is the resurrection of Jesus from the dead. By raising Jesus from the dead, God declared to the world that He had accepted Jesus' sacrifice on our behalf.

If Jesus had remained in the grave, we would have seen that he was just another sinful human being like us. His death would have been worthless. He would have died for his own sins, not ours. As the Bible states, without the resurrection, we would have no hope, "And if Christ is not risen, your faith is futile; you are still in your sins." (1Corinthians 15:17)

The resurrection shows that death could not keep its hold on Jesus. It shows that God, the Judge, considered our penalty to have been paid. Our sins had been dealt with. Jesus broke the death barrier.

Anyone who has said goodbye to a departed loved one at a graveside knows that death is a formidable enemy. Yet, for Christians facing death, there is the certainty of eternal life beyond the grave. This certainty comes from the knowledge that Jesus Christ overcame death and its sting. Jesus did this through His triumphant resurrection. "Death is swallowed up in victory. O Death, where is your sting?" (1Corinthians 15:54-55)

If Jesus died on the cross, and if Jesus is God, does that mean that God died on the cross?

God is Spirit. In the original Hebrew language, Spirit is *roh.* From this word, the word *rihe* is taken, which means "the air". We can say, therefore, that God's Spirit is like the air in the atmosphere. Air is everywhere. Though you cannot see it, you know it is present: you can feel it, you breathe it, even though it has no colour or shape. Similarly, the Spirit of God is present everywhere.

An empty bottle does not contain any liquid, but you know that it is full of air. The air inside the bottle has taken the shape of the bottle, even though air has no shape. The characteristics of the air inside the bottle are similar to the characteristics of the air outside the bottle. The fact that there is air inside the bottle does not mean that there is no air outside the bottle! Now, if you were to take the bottle and smash it against a wall, it would break into hundreds of pieces. It would be shattered. Could we say that the air inside the bottle would also be shattered? No. Only the form that contained the air would have been shattered.

A similar thing took place when God, who is Spirit, dwelt among us in the body of Jesus Christ. God took the likeness of man. That did not mean that He no longer existed elsewhere. Like the air when it filled the bottle, God still existed everywhere. Furthermore, Jesus' crucifixion did not mean that God was killed, but rather that the human body which contained the Spirit of God was killed. God always lived, even during the three days when Jesus was dead in the tomb.

I am so bad. God could never be interested in me!

When we look up at the stars and consider how vast the universe is we realize, to a small degree, how great God is. And we ask, "Can the Great God, who made and sustains millions of stars, ever look at someone as small as I am? How could He care for me or hear my prayers? Surely God is too great to be interested in the affairs of individuals among the billions of people on this earth?"

Let us consider how Jesus treated individual people. Was He too great to be concerned about the joys and sorrows of ordinary people? By no means! On the contrary, we see that Jesus Christ had love and sympathy for every person He met. He wanted to give health and happiness and salvation to each one. Thousands of people came to Jesus for help: rich and poor, old and young, men and women, His own people and foreigners... no one was turned away. For Jesus said, "the one who comes to Me I will by no means cast away" (Bible, John 6:37).

Jesus the friend of sinners!

We have all sinned against God. God could have destroyed us. But when we become acquainted with Jesus, the perfect manifestation of God, we are surprised to see that He does not hate sinners. Instead of condemning or avoiding them, Jesus often ate in their homes and showed them great kindness. For this strange conduct He was severely criticized by the religious leaders of the people, who called Him "*the friend of sinners.*" Jesus replied that these sinners were sick, and He was their physician. As the doctor does not wish to kill his patient but to make him well, so God does not want sinners to perish but to be saved. He came to seek and to save those who had lost the way and were dying in their sin.

Can Jesus have time for a sinner like me?

In case you still doubt whether God is interested in you, let me tell you about the first people Jesus appeared to after He rose from the dead.

The first person who saw the risen Jesus was a nobody! Her name was Mary Magdalene. She had once been demon possessed. Presumably she had lived the worst sort of life as a result. She was a nobody, but Jesus met her. Why? Because **Jesus has time for nobodies.**

Later that day Jesus appeared to a failure. One of His disciples had denied Him three times in one night although he had said he would not. Jesus forgave this sorrowful man because **Jesus Christ has time for failures.**

On the same day He appeared to people who were confused. They were walking, and they could not understand the events which had happened in the last few days. How could Jesus have been crucified? They had loved Him so much. They had heard reports that He had been raised from the dead and they were perplexed. Then Jesus walked with them, because **He has time for people who are confused.**

There were also ten disciples who were so afraid that they locked the doors. Jesus did not unlock the doors. He just went in and stood where they were. Why did He meet them? Because **He has time for fearful people too**.

Then, there was one disciple who could not believe that Jesus had been raised from the dead. How did Jesus react to his doubts? Did he condemn the man? No! He went to meet him, because **Jesus Christ has time for doubters**!

Then there was a cynic, a man who had lived in the same house as Jesus in Nazareth, His half brother James. Throughout all those years he had not believed a word of what Jesus had said. His only comment on the situation had been that Jesus was mad. Yet Jesus met James and brought him to be a believer, because **Jesus has time for cynics!**

There was also one man who met Jesus a little later. He was a great opponent to Christianity, seeking to imprison and kill Christians. Do you know how Jesus treated him? As this man Saul was going on a death mission to Damascus to kill as many Christians as possible, Jesus met him in the middle of his sin! He said, 'Saul, Saul why are you persecuting Me?' Saul was converted, because **Jesus Christ even has time for His opponents.**

And so to the question: "Does God care for individuals?" We confidently reply, "Yes He does! Look at Jesus Christ who is the image and revelation of the invisible God." There is no class of people for whom Jesus Christ has no time. 'For God so loved the world that He gave His only begotten Son (Jesus), that whoever *[and you can put your name right here, right now]* believes in him should not perish, but have everlasting life' (Bible, John 3:16).

So, how can I know God personally?

In conclusion, we ask again, 'How can a man know God?' The answer is: through Creation, the Bible, and Jesus Christ.

However, God is not content that we should simply have accurate information about Him. He wants us to reach the point where He is no longer a stranger to us. He wants us to love Him with all our heart and soul. You may know things about God, but what is more important is to know Him personally and intimately as your Father. This can only happen when you entrust yourself to the Lord Jesus Christ and receive Him into your life.

The way is open for you. Jesus invites you to come to Him and meet God face to face. Do you really want to find God? Then accept Christ's invitation and believe in Him. "You will seek Me and find *Me*, when you search for Me with all your heart. I will be found by you, says the LORD," (Bible, Jeremiah 29:13, 14).

You can receive Jesus into your life now by talking to Him sincerely in prayer. Open your heart to Him, acknowledge and confess your sins. Ask God to wash you from your sins by the blood that Jesus spilt on the cross. God forgives those who humble themselves before Him in this way. He is perfectly aware of all that is in your heart, so it is useless trying to hide anything. Acknowledge God's right to reign in your life. Ask Him to make you into the person He wants you to be.

I encourage you to take God's Holy Word (the Bible) very seriously. Don't let anything stop you putting right your relationship with God.

You may like to pray something like this:

> **"Dear God, I confess I am a sinner. Thank You that Jesus took my punishment upon Himself when He died on the cross for my sins, and then rose from the dead, defeating death. Today, I repent and place my trust in Jesus Christ alone for my salvation. In Jesus' name I pray. Amen."**

The Bible promises, "as many as received Him (Jesus Christ), to them He gave the right to become children of God, to those who believe in His name" (Bible, John 1:12).

[1] God called Himself 'I am'. The phrase refers not only to His eternal existence, without beginning or end, but to the fact that He is dependent on nothing and no-one else for His existence.

[2] If you want to know more about the deity of Jesus, read E.M. Hicham's book entitled, 'Who is this Jesus?'

If you would like to receive further information, please contact us.

If you wish to make further study of the Christian faith, correspondence courses in English, Arabic and French are available from:

Word of Hope Ministries
22 New Street,
Rochdale,
OL16 3PQ,
United Kingdom

Email: **word.hope@gmail.com**
Web: **www.word-of-hope.net**

To find out more

Jesus-Islam.org
A website for Christian-Muslim discussion and apologetics